Shirley Barber's
FAIRY BOOK
An Anthology of Verse

Dalmatian Press

Shirley Barber's
FAIRY BOOK
An Anthology of Verse

First Published by The Five Mile Press Pty Ltd 1995
Copyright © Marbit Pty Ltd

Text and illustrations by Shirley Barber

Published in the United States in 2004 by Dalmatian Press, LLC.
The DALMATIAN PRESS name and logo are trademarks of
Dalmatian Press, Franklin, Tennessee, 37067
ISBN: 1-40371-198-4
13810-1004

Printed in Hong Kong

04 05 06 07 10 9 8 7 6 5 4 3 2 1

Contents

The Fairy's Tree

I've never seen a fairy,
But I know just where she'd hide.
I'm sure I've found her hollow tree
'Cos when I peep inside
I see a cobweb cover,
Moss pillow for her head,
A little glowworm night-light—
(I think she reads in bed!)
There's her toadstool table,
And on it I can see
A gummut cup and saucer
For her morning cup of tea.
I think the fairy's hiding
In the shadows out of sight.
I'll go back home to dinner now
And to her I will write
A teeny-weeny letter,
And this is what I'll say —
"I'd love to meet you, Fairy,
Will you please come out and play?"

Shirley Barber

Toadstools

It's not a bit windy,
It's not a bit wet,
The sky is as sunny
As summer, and yet
Little umbrellas are
Everywhere spread:
Pink ones, and brown ones,
And orange, and red.

I can't see the folks
Who are hidden below;
I've peeped, and I've peeped
Round the edges—but no!
They hold their umbrellas
So tight and so close
That nothing shows under,
Not even a nose!

Elizabeth Fleming

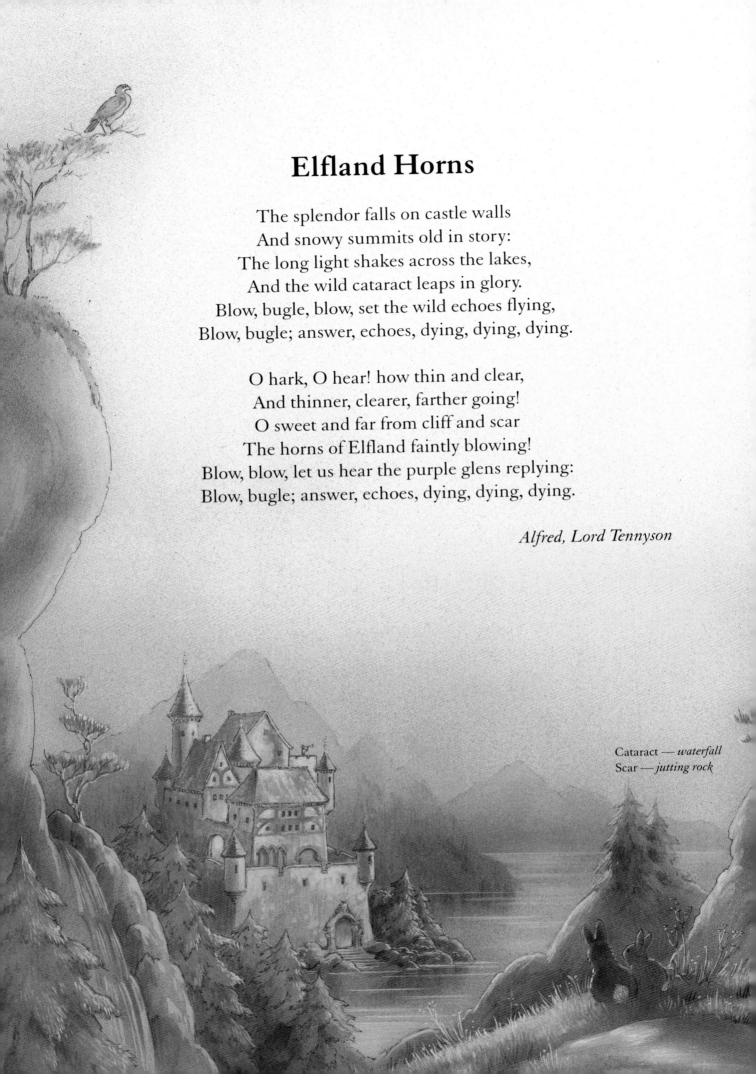

Elfland Horns

The splendor falls on castle walls
And snowy summits old in story:
The long light shakes across the lakes,
And the wild cataract leaps in glory.
Blow, bugle, blow, set the wild echoes flying,
Blow, bugle; answer, echoes, dying, dying, dying.

O hark, O hear! how thin and clear,
And thinner, clearer, farther going!
O sweet and far from cliff and scar
The horns of Elfland faintly blowing!
Blow, blow, let us hear the purple glens replying:
Blow, bugle; answer, echoes, dying, dying, dying.

Alfred, Lord Tennyson

Cataract — *waterfall*
Scar — *jutting rock*

The Fairies

Up the airy mountain,
    Down the rushy glen,
We daren't go a-hunting
    For fear of little men.
Wee folk, good folk,
    Trooping all together;
Green jacket, red cap,
    And white owl's feather!

Down along the rocky shore
    Some make their home.
They live on crispy pancakes
    Of yellow tide-foam;
Some in the reeds
    Of the black mountain lake,
With frogs for their watchdogs,
    All night awake.

William Allingham

Bedtime Story

Tell me my favorite story
While I am snuggling down,
About the beautiful fairy
Who wears a sparkling gown.

Tell me about her silken hair,
Her rainbow-colored wings.
Tell of her bag of magic stars;
Sing me the song she sings.

Tell me she flies through the forest dark
And after a while she hears
A poor little bunny crying,
So, gently she dries his tears.

She carries him home to his burrow
So he's just in time for tea.
(His mother was looking out for him
Just as you look for me!)

For an hour or so she lingers.
She sings the bunny to sleep,
Then leaves behind on his pillow
A magical star to keep.

I'll help you remember the wording.
It has to be told just right.
And then you can tell me it all again
Tomorrow — and every night!

Shirley Barber

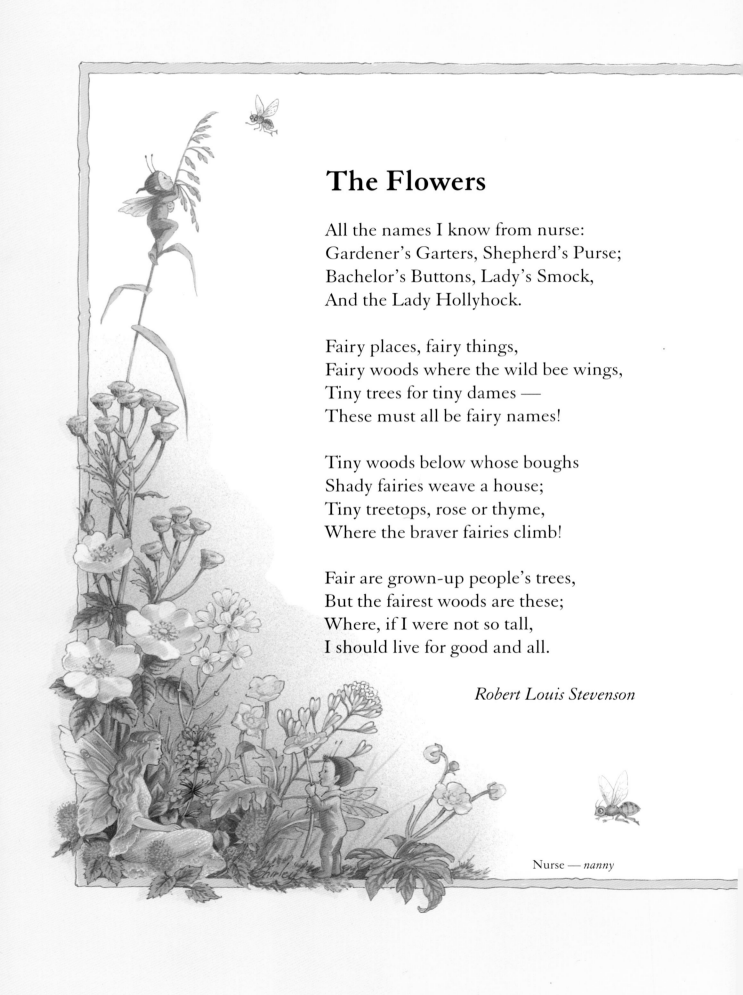

The Flowers

All the names I know from nurse:
Gardener's Garters, Shepherd's Purse;
Bachelor's Buttons, Lady's Smock,
And the Lady Hollyhock.

Fairy places, fairy things,
Fairy woods where the wild bee wings,
Tiny trees for tiny dames —
These must all be fairy names!

Tiny woods below whose boughs
Shady fairies weave a house;
Tiny treetops, rose or thyme,
Where the braver fairies climb!

Fair are grown-up people's trees,
But the fairest woods are these;
Where, if I were not so tall,
I should live for good and all.

Robert Louis Stevenson

Nurse — *nanny*

The Miniature World

If I was very, very small
The jointed grasses would be tall,
And I would climb them, just like trees,
To wave to passing honey bees.
And then I think I'd like to try
To ride a big blue dragonfly —
Zigzag around the sky like mad
Then land it on a lily pad.
When I was hungry I would eat
Sorrel, mint and meadowsweet.
Maybe I'd leapfrog real frogs,
Or maybe dive off mossy logs
Into pools deep, cool and dim,
And with the little tadpoles swim.
Of course, it would be very scary
Meeting spiders, black and hairy!
And those giant drops of dew —
I guess I'd have to dodge them too!
But it would be so nice to know
The hidden paths where Fairies go,
And oh! so good to spend my days
Exploring secret forest ways . . .
And when I was too tired to roam
I'd hail a beetle and ride home!

Shirley Barber

The Fairies' Ball

Katie has a fine doll's house,
It stands against the wall;
Her grandma gave it to her and
It's elegant and tall.

Katie said, at midnight,
Or perhaps a little after,
She was woken by the tiny sounds
Of music and of laughter.

She sat up in her bed and thought
She really must be dreaming —
From every little doll's house window
Golden light was streaming.

She crept across to see what could
Be going on in there,
And saw it was a fairies' ball —
A very grand affair.

All night the fairies reveled, then,
At dawn, away they flew.
Now Katie's just a little cross
At all there is to do.

She doesn't mind her doll's house used
By fairies and by elves,
But thinks that they should always
Clean up afterward themselves!

Shirley Barber

The Fairy Market

My grandma, when a little child,
One silver moonlit night,
Climbed up the hill behind her home
And saw a magic sight;
Among the tangled rowan trees
Within a ferny dell,
A crowd of fairy folk had come,
Their goods to buy and sell.
Bright lanterns lit the market stalls
Whereon lay lovely things:
Gleaming wands and cobweb shawls,
Necklaces and rings,
Elfin caps and buckled shoes,
Berries, fruit and bread —
"And then I saw this silver chain
And loved it," Grandma said.
"So out I bravely stepped and went
Into the fairy throng.
I bought the chain — will you believe? —
It only cost a song!"

Shirley Barber

Rowan — *ash tree*
Dell — *small valley*

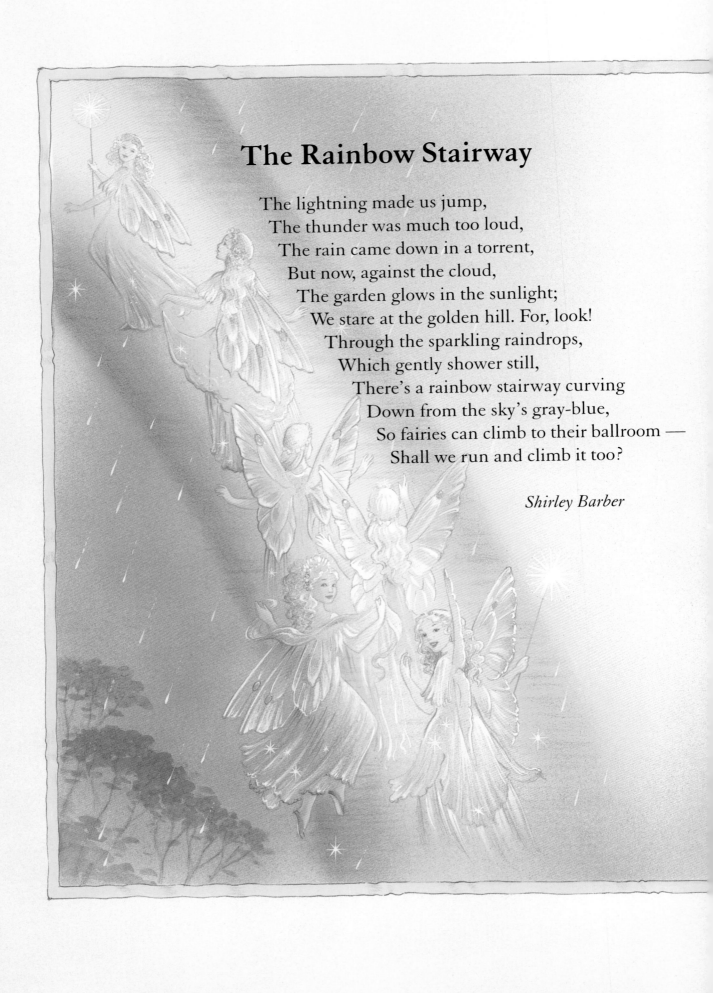

The Rainbow Stairway

The lightning made us jump,
The thunder was much too loud,
The rain came down in a torrent,
But now, against the cloud,
The garden glows in the sunlight;
We stare at the golden hill. For, look!
Through the sparkling raindrops,
Which gently shower still,
There's a rainbow stairway curving
Down from the sky's gray-blue,
So fairies can climb to their ballroom —
Shall we run and climb it too?

Shirley Barber

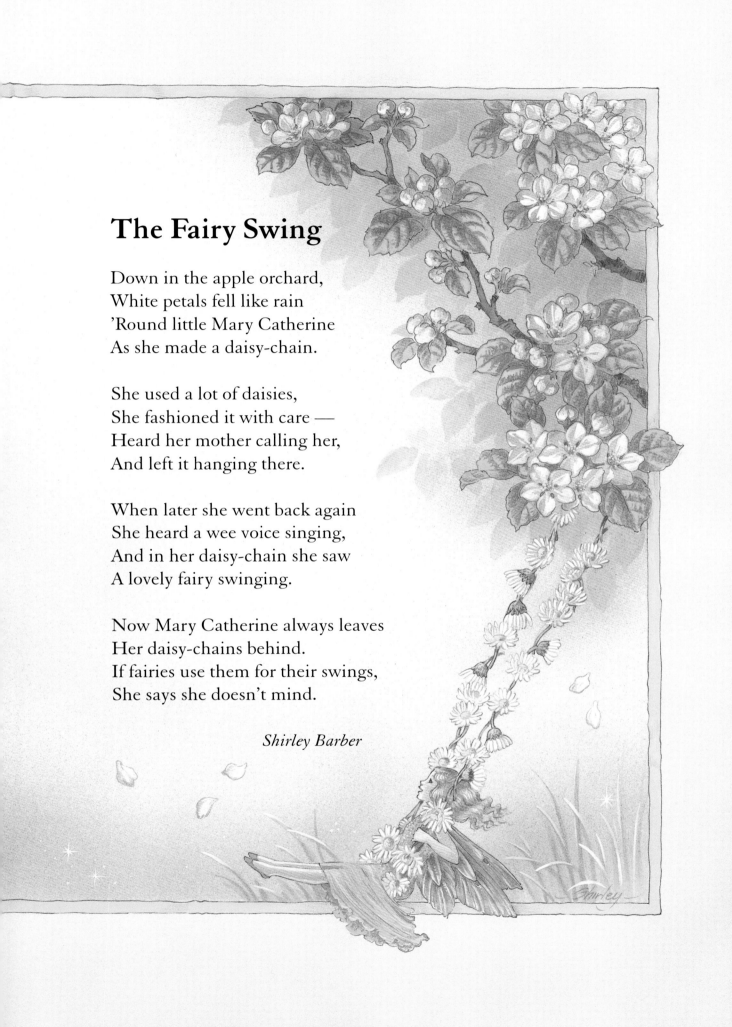

The Fairy Swing

Down in the apple orchard,
White petals fell like rain
'Round little Mary Catherine
As she made a daisy-chain.

She used a lot of daisies,
She fashioned it with care —
Heard her mother calling her,
And left it hanging there.

When later she went back again
She heard a wee voice singing,
And in her daisy-chain she saw
A lovely fairy swinging.

Now Mary Catherine always leaves
Her daisy-chains behind.
If fairies use them for their swings,
She says she doesn't mind.

Shirley Barber

Elfin Friends

Uncle William knew an elf,
"A manikin," he said,
"In pointed hat and buckled shoes
And a suit of green and red."

Aunt Betty knew an elf
Of whom she grew quite fond.
They quareled when he tried to fish
The goldfish from her pond.

My grandma said a little elf
She often used to see.
He'd visit her to chat and drink
A thimbleful of tea.

She knitted him a woolly cap
With flaps to warm his ears,
And he was very grateful —
They were friends for years and years.

"They teach you silly things," she said,
"When first you go to school,
Like knitting useless woolly snakes
Right through a wooden spool"

But I had such a good idea!
In red and green and white
I've knitted socks for chilly elves —
(I hope they're not *too* bright!)

If I can stay awake tonight,
And if there is an elf,
And if he likes his socks, I'll have
An elfin friend myself.

Shirley Barber

The Little Elfman

I met a little elfman once,
Down where the lilies blow.
I asked him why he was so small,
And why he didn't grow.

He slightly frowned, and with his eye
He looked me through and through —
"I'm just as big for me," said he,
"As you are big for you!"

John Kendrick Bangs

The Tea Party

A robin brought the message —
She'll come at half-past three.
We'll sit where it is shady
Beneath the willow tree.
I'll make some tiny sandwiches,
Fill flower cups with dew.
A pollen cake I'll try to make
And daisy biscuits too.
I'll lay upon this toadstool
Rose petal plates for three.
The table must look pretty when
A Fairy comes to tea.

Shirley Barber

The Fairy Queen

The woodland is hushed —
It seems to be waiting.
Even the breeze doesn't stir.
Everything seems to be anticipating
A wonderful thing to occur.
Through bluebells and ferns
A green pathway is wending;
Rabbits each side of it sit.
Above them the blossom boughs
Downward are bending
Where small birds excitedly flit.
Hark! there's the sound of a
Small drummer drumming.
Rabbits respectfully stand.
Now down the pathway
They're coming! They're coming!
A colorful miniature band!
The mice shake the bluebells
And they begin ringing —
The tiniest tinkling sound.
Now come the baby elves
Hopping and springing
Over the soft mossy ground.
And here are the fairies,
(Oh, can I be dreaming?) —
Some flying, some dancing along.
In jewel-bright garments
Aglitter and gleaming,
They sing such a haunting, sweet song.
And lastly, the fairest,
Her delicate dress is
Oh, shimmering gold and pale green;
A diamond crown on her
Floating silk tresses —
The beautiful Fairy Queen!

Shirley Barber

Fairy Dresses

The other day I woke at dawn
And tiptoed out onto the lawn,
Then I stared in such surprise
At the sight which met my eyes.
Everywhere I looked there were
Veils of jeweled gossamer.
Where the hollyhocks grow tall
Fairy shawls lay over all;
On the rose-arch, in each space,
Petticoats of finest lace.
On the lupins and the phlox
Hung the daintiest fairy frocks,
Diamond-sprinkled, shimmering,
And, in shadows glimmering,
Sequinned cloaks for evening wear;
Twinkling strands for golden hair.
Someone (hiding I suppose)
Must have fashioned all those clothes,
Hoped a fairy passing by
Would fly down, her dress to buy.
But — whose fingers, small but strong,
Had been so busy all night long?

Shirley Barber

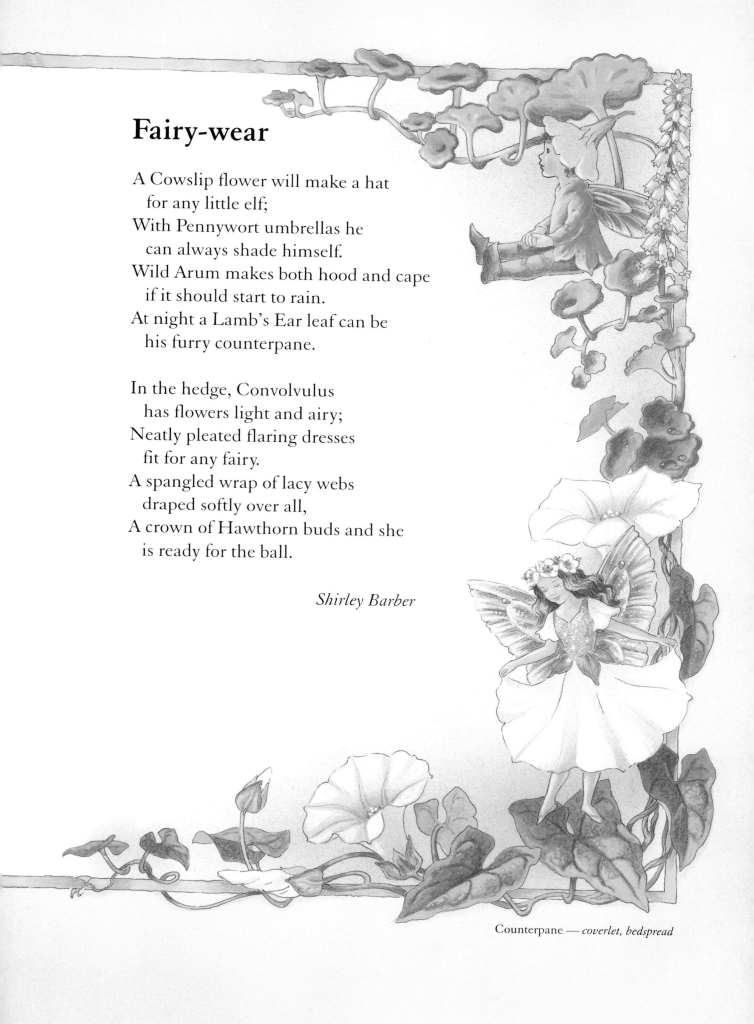

Fairy-wear

A Cowslip flower will make a hat
  for any little elf;
With Pennywort umbrellas he
  can always shade himself.
Wild Arum makes both hood and cape
  if it should start to rain.
At night a Lamb's Ear leaf can be
  his furry counterpane.

In the hedge, Convolvulus
  has flowers light and airy;
Neatly pleated flaring dresses
  fit for any fairy.
A spangled wrap of lacy webs
  draped softly over all,
A crown of Hawthorn buds and she
  is ready for the ball.

Shirley Barber

Counterpane — *coverlet, bedspread*

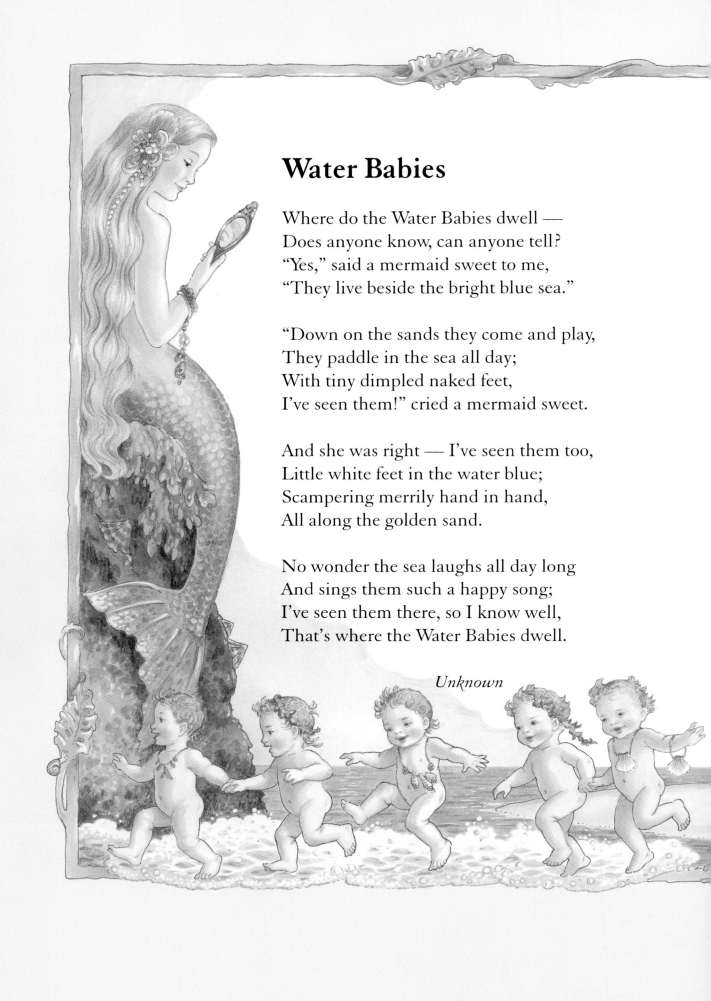

Water Babies

Where do the Water Babies dwell —
Does anyone know, can anyone tell?
"Yes," said a mermaid sweet to me,
"They live beside the bright blue sea."

"Down on the sands they come and play,
They paddle in the sea all day;
With tiny dimpled naked feet,
I've seen them!" cried a mermaid sweet.

And she was right — I've seen them too,
Little white feet in the water blue;
Scampering merrily hand in hand,
All along the golden sand.

No wonder the sea laughs all day long
And sings them such a happy song;
I've seen them there, so I know well,
That's where the Water Babies dwell.

Unknown

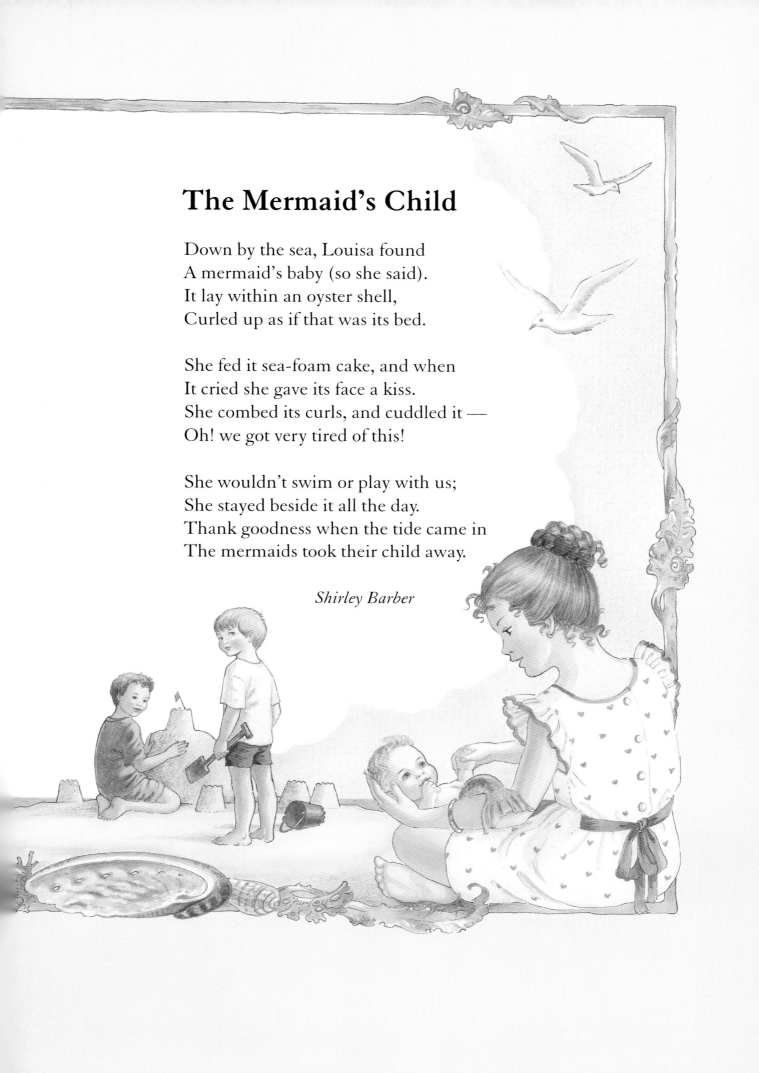

The Mermaid's Child

Down by the sea, Louisa found
A mermaid's baby (so she said).
It lay within an oyster shell,
Curled up as if that was its bed.

She fed it sea-foam cake, and when
It cried she gave its face a kiss.
She combed its curls, and cuddled it —
Oh! we got very tired of this!

She wouldn't swim or play with us;
She stayed beside it all the day.
Thank goodness when the tide came in
The mermaids took their child away.

Shirley Barber

The Dream Fairy

A little fairy comes at night —
Her eyes are blue, her hair is brown,
With silver spots upon her wings —
And from the moon she flutters down.

She has a little silver wand,
And when a good child goes to bed
She waves her wand from right to left
And makes a circle round its head.

And then it dreams of pleasant things —
Of fountains filled with fairy fish,
And trees that bear delicious fruit
And bow their branches at a wish;

Of arbors filled with dainty scents
From lovely flowers that never fade,
Bright 'flies that flitter in the sun,
And glowworms shining in the shade;

And talking birds with gifted tongues
For singing songs and telling tales,
And pretty dwarfs to show the way
Through fairy hills and fairy dales.

Thomas Hood

The Fairy Folk

Come cuddle close in Daddy's coat
Beside the fire so bright,
And hear about the fairy folk
That wander in the night.
For when the stars are shining clear
And all the world is still,
They float across the silver moon
From hill to cloudy hill.

Their caps of red, their cloaks of green,
Are hung with silver bells,
And when they're shaken with the wind
Their merry ringing swells.
And riding on the crimson moth,
With black spots on her wings,
They guide them down the purple sky
With golden bridle rings.

They love to visit girls and boys
To see how sweet they sleep,
To stand beside their cozy cots
And at their faces peep.
For in the whole of Fairyland
They have no finer sight
Than little children sleeping sound
With faces rosy bright.

Robert M. Bird

The Fairy Book

In summer, when the grass is thick,
  if Mother has the time,
She shows me with her pencil how
  a poet makes a rhyme.
And often she is sweet enough
  to choose a leafy nook,
Where I cuddle up so closely
  when she reads the Fairy book.

In winter, when the corn's asleep,
  and birds are not in song,
And crocuses and violets have
  been away too long,
Dear mother puts her thimble by
  in an answer to my look,
And I cuddle up so closely when
  she reads the Fairy book.

Norman Gale

The Little Folk

In Spring, when the cherry-plum blossom
Lay soft as pink foam in the trees,
I saw them descend on the garden.
At first, sure, I thought it was bees!

Down where the petals were scattered,
Laughing and singing they came.
I watched from my window astonished —
The Little Folk playing a game.

They swung from the flower-laden branches.
They twisted and spun on the wing.
Their singing was sweeter than silver
As they sang and they danced in a ring.

Well! I never saw a sight like it —
The Little Folk all at their play.
Then Pussycat pounced from the bushes,
And up they all flew — and away!

Shirley Barber

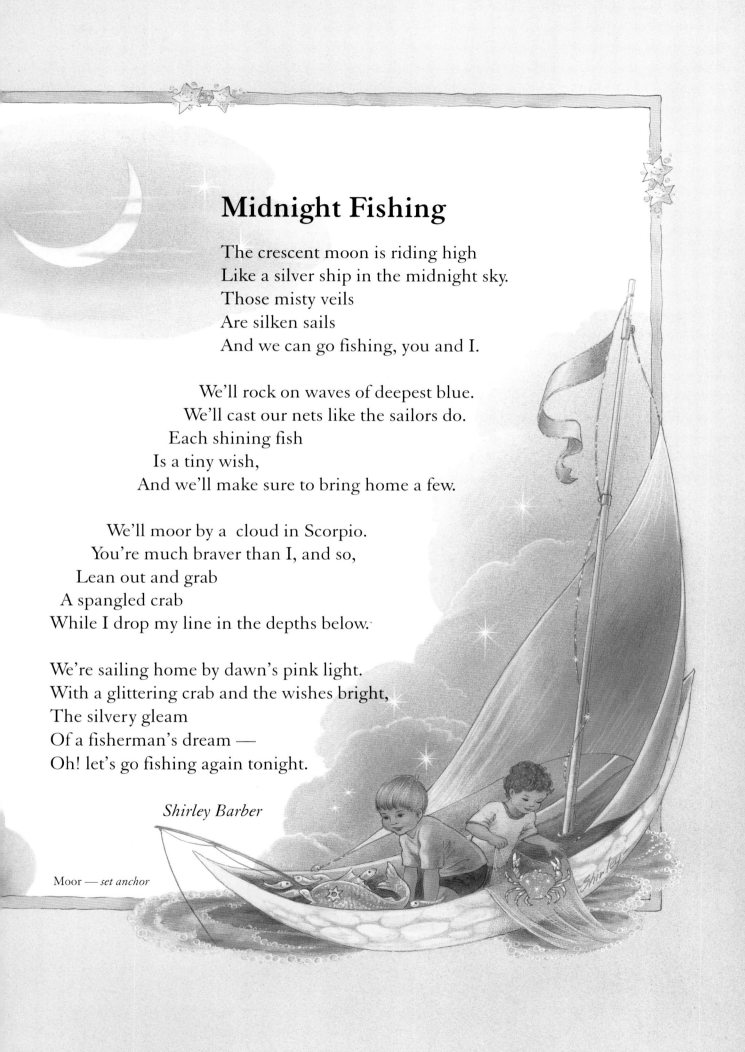

Midnight Fishing

The crescent moon is riding high
Like a silver ship in the midnight sky.
Those misty veils
Are silken sails
And we can go fishing, you and I.

We'll rock on waves of deepest blue.
We'll cast our nets like the sailors do.
Each shining fish
Is a tiny wish,
And we'll make sure to bring home a few.

We'll moor by a cloud in Scorpio.
You're much braver than I, and so,
Lean out and grab
A spangled crab
While I drop my line in the depths below.

We're sailing home by dawn's pink light.
With a glittering crab and the wishes bright,
The silvery gleam
Of a fisherman's dream —
Oh! let's go fishing again tonight.

Shirley Barber

Moor — *set anchor*

Twelve O'clock — Fairy-time

Through the house give glimmering light
By the dead and drowsy fire;
Every elf and fairy sprite
Hop as light as bird from brier.

. . . .

Now, until the break of day,
Through this house each fairy stray . . .

William Shakespeare